Today I Feel...

a

Workbook

TODAY I FEEL... A DoodlyCouch© Drawing Therapy Journal

Today I Feel...
A DoodlyCouch Workbook
Copyright 2009
Amy S. Morgan
Photocopying and reproduction prohibited

TODAY I FEEL... A DoodlyCouch© Drawing Therapy Journal

How do you feel today?

Talking about feelings can be hard sometimes. Writing can also be hard, because we try too hard to find just the right words.

Drawing and art therapy have been used for years as a way to enable kids and adults to express their feelings without the limitations of words.

This workbook has been designed as a way to explore feelings, in a creative and expressive way, without judgment or a "right or wrong" answer. Each page asks a simple question, and then leaves open space for drawing any feelings or thoughts related to the question. The process of drawing feelings out may provide its own healing, or may reveal some areas where there is a need to explore and seek further help from a qualified professional.

TODAY I FEEL... A DoodlyCouch© Drawing Therapy Journal

Disclaimer

Questions presented in the Workbook are presented solely for the purpose of inspiring the reader to draw about his or her own feelings on the topics. This workbook should not be used to diagnose or prescribe treatment for any illness or disorder for a particular individual. It is not intended to replace the advice of psychiatrists, psychologists, therapists, physicians or health care practitioners and should not be used in place of a visit, call or consultation or the advice of a qualified care provider. The workbook in no way provides medical or counseling advice. If, after drawing in this workbook, you feel that you or your child need help with a particular topic or area, we recommend seeking professional guidance and care from a qualified practitioner.

This workbook, the author, and sponsoring company and publisher make no claim, guarantee or warranty as to the results that may be obtained from using the workbook. The Workbook, nor any of its authors, contributors, or other representatives will be liable for damages arising out of or in connection with the use of the workbook. This applies to all damages of any kind, including (without limitation) compensatory, direct, indirect or consequential damages, loss of data, income or profit, loss of or damage to property and claims of third parties. Your use of the Workbook confirms your agreement of the terms and conditions described herein. If you do not agree, you will not utilize the Workbook.

Copyrights, Trademarks & Credits

Unless otherwise indicated, all information in the Workbook is Copyright ©2009 Corporate Elements, LLC and Amy S. Morgan. All rights reserved. Any unauthorized copying or reproduction of any of the content in any form is strictly prohibited.

Contacting Corporate Elements, LLC
If you have any questions about this document, please contact:

Amy S. Morgan
Doodlycouch Workbooks
Corporate Elements, LLC
Amy@CorpElements.com
www.CorpElements.com
Phone (405) 326-4116

TODAY I FEEL... A DoodlyCouch© Drawing Therapy Journal

Date:_____

How do you feel today?
Take as much time as you'd like, and either draw or write about your feelings today:

TODAY I FEEL... A DoodlyCouch© Drawing Therapy Journal

Date:_____

How do you feel today?
Take as much time as you'd like, and either draw or write about your feelings today:

TODAY I FEEL... A DoodlyCouch© Drawing Therapy Journal

Date:_____

How do you feel today?
Take as much time as you'd like, and either draw or write about your feelings today:

TODAY I FEEL... A DoodlyCouch© Drawing Therapy Journal

Date:_____

How do you feel today?
Take as much time as you'd like, and either draw or write about your feelings today:

TODAY I FEEL... A DoodlyCouch© Drawing Therapy Journal

Date:_____

How do you feel today?
Take as much time as you'd like, and either draw or write about your feelings today:

TODAY I FEEL... A DoodlyCouch© Drawing Therapy Journal

Date:_____

How do you feel today?
Take as much time as you'd like, and either draw or write about your feelings today:

TODAY I FEEL... A DoodlyCouch© Drawing Therapy Journal

Date:_____

How do you feel today?
Take as much time as you'd like, and either draw or write about your feelings today:

TODAY I FEEL... A DoodlyCouch© Drawing Therapy Journal

Date:_____

How do you feel today?
Take as much time as you'd like, and either draw or write about your feelings today:

TODAY I FEEL... A DoodlyCouch© Drawing Therapy Journal

Date:_____

How do you feel today?
Take as much time as you'd like, and either draw or write about your feelings today:

TODAY I FEEL... A DoodlyCouch© Drawing Therapy Journal

Date:_____

How do you feel today?
Take as much time as you'd like, and either draw or write about your feelings today:

TODAY I FEEL... A DoodlyCouch© Drawing Therapy Journal

Date:_____

How do you feel today?
Take as much time as you'd like, and either draw or write about your feelings today:

TODAY I FEEL... A DoodlyCouch© Drawing Therapy Journal

Date:_____

How do you feel today?
Take as much time as you'd like, and either draw or write about your feelings today:

TODAY I FEEL… A DoodlyCouch© Drawing Therapy Journal

Date:_____

How do you feel today?
Take as much time as you'd like, and either draw or write about your feelings today:

TODAY I FEEL... A DoodlyCouch© Drawing Therapy Journal

Date:_____

How do you feel today?
Take as much time as you'd like, and either draw or write about your feelings today:

TODAY I FEEL... A DoodlyCouch© Drawing Therapy Journal

Date:_____

How do you feel today?
Take as much time as you'd like, and either draw or write about your feelings today:

TODAY I FEEL... A DoodlyCouch© Drawing Therapy Journal

Date:_____

How do you feel today?
Take as much time as you'd like, and either draw or write about your feelings today:

TODAY I FEEL... A DoodlyCouch© Drawing Therapy Journal

Date:_____

How do you feel today?
Take as much time as you'd like, and either draw or write about your feelings today:

TODAY I FEEL... A DoodlyCouch© Drawing Therapy Journal

Date:_____

How do you feel today?
Take as much time as you'd like, and either draw or write about your feelings today:

TODAY I FEEL... A DoodlyCouch© Drawing Therapy Journal

Date:_____

How do you feel today?

Take as much time as you'd like, and either draw or write about your feelings today:

TODAY I FEEL... A DoodlyCouch© Drawing Therapy Journal

Date:_____

How do you feel today?
Take as much time as you'd like, and either draw or write about your feelings today:

TODAY I FEEL... A DoodlyCouch© Drawing Therapy Journal

Date:_____

How do you feel today?

Take as much time as you'd like, and either draw or write about your feelings today:

TODAY I FEEL... A DoodlyCouch© Drawing Therapy Journal

Date:_____

How do you feel today?
Take as much time as you'd like, and either draw or write about your feelings today:

TODAY I FEEL... A DoodlyCouch© Drawing Therapy Journal

Date:_____

How do you feel today?
Take as much time as you'd like, and either draw or write about your feelings today:

TODAY I FEEL... A DoodlyCouch© Drawing Therapy Journal

Date:_____

How do you feel today?

Take as much time as you'd like, and either draw or write about your feelings today:

TODAY I FEEL... A DoodlyCouch© Drawing Therapy Journal

Date:_____

How do you feel today?

Take as much time as you'd like, and either draw or write about your feelings today:

TODAY I FEEL... A DoodlyCouch© Drawing Therapy Journal

Date:_____

How do you feel today?
Take as much time as you'd like, and either draw or write about your feelings today:

TODAY I FEEL… A DoodlyCouch© Drawing Therapy Journal

Date:_____

How do you feel today?

Take as much time as you'd like, and either draw or write about your feelings today:

TODAY I FEEL... A DoodlyCouch© Drawing Therapy Journal

Date:_____

How do you feel today?
Take as much time as you'd like, and either draw or write about your feelings today:

TODAY I FEEL... A DoodlyCouch© Drawing Therapy Journal

Date:_____

How do you feel today?

Take as much time as you'd like, and either draw or write about your feelings today:

TODAY I FEEL... A DoodlyCouch© Drawing Therapy Journal

Date:_____

How do you feel today?
Take as much time as you'd like, and either draw or write about your feelings today:

TODAY I FEEL... A DoodlyCouch© Drawing Therapy Journal

Date:_____

How do you feel today?
Take as much time as you'd like, and either draw or write about your feelings today:

TODAY I FEEL... A DoodlyCouch© Drawing Therapy Journal

Date:_____

How do you feel today?

Take as much time as you'd like, and either draw or write about your feelings today:

TODAY I FEEL... A DoodlyCouch© Drawing Therapy Journal

Date:_____

How do you feel today?
Take as much time as you'd like, and either draw or write about your feelings today:

TODAY I FEEL... A DoodlyCouch© Drawing Therapy Journal

Date:_____

How do you feel today?
Take as much time as you'd like, and either draw or write about your feelings today:

TODAY I FEEL... A DoodlyCouch© Drawing Therapy Journal

Date:_____

How do you feel today?
Take as much time as you'd like, and either draw or write about your feelings today:

TODAY I FEEL... A DoodlyCouch© Drawing Therapy Journal

Date:_____

How do you feel today?
Take as much time as you'd like, and either draw or write about your feelings today:

TODAY I FEEL... A DoodlyCouch© Drawing Therapy Journal

Date:_____

How do you feel today?

Take as much time as you'd like, and either draw or write about your feelings today:

TODAY I FEEL... A DoodlyCouch© Drawing Therapy Journal

Date:_____

How do you feel today?
Take as much time as you'd like, and either draw or write about your feelings today:

TODAY I FEEL... A DoodlyCouch© Drawing Therapy Journal

Date:_____

How do you feel today?
Take as much time as you'd like, and either draw or write about your feelings today:

TODAY I FEEL... A DoodlyCouch© Drawing Therapy Journal

Date:_____

How do you feel today?
Take as much time as you'd like, and either draw or write about your feelings today:

TODAY I FEEL... A DoodlyCouch© Drawing Therapy Journal

Date:_____

How do you feel today?
Take as much time as you'd like, and either draw or write about your feelings today:

TODAY I FEEL... A DoodlyCouch© Drawing Therapy Journal

Date:_____

How do you feel today?
Take as much time as you'd like, and either draw or write about your feelings today:

TODAY I FEEL... A DoodlyCouch© Drawing Therapy Journal

Date:_____

How do you feel today?
Take as much time as you'd like, and either draw or write about your feelings today:

TODAY I FEEL... A DoodlyCouch© Drawing Therapy Journal

Date:_____

How do you feel today?
Take as much time as you'd like, and either draw or write about your feelings today:

TODAY I FEEL... A DoodlyCouch© Drawing Therapy Journal

Date:_____

How do you feel today?
Take as much time as you'd like, and either draw or write about your feelings today:

TODAY I FEEL... A DoodlyCouch© Drawing Therapy Journal

Date:_____

How do you feel today?
Take as much time as you'd like, and either draw or write about your feelings today:

TODAY I FEEL... A DoodlyCouch© Drawing Therapy Journal

Date:_____

How do you feel today?
Take as much time as you'd like, and either draw or write about your feelings today:

TODAY I FEEL... A DoodlyCouch© Drawing Therapy Journal

Date:_____

How do you feel today?
Take as much time as you'd like, and either draw or write about your feelings today:

TODAY I FEEL… A DoodlyCouch© Drawing Therapy Journal

Date:_____

How do you feel today?
Take as much time as you'd like, and either draw or write about your feelings today:

TODAY I FEEL... A DoodlyCouch© Drawing Therapy Journal

Date:_____

How do you feel today?
Take as much time as you'd like, and either draw or write about your feelings today:

TODAY I FEEL... A DoodlyCouch© Drawing Therapy Journal

Date:_____

How do you feel today?

Take as much time as you'd like, and either draw or write about your feelings today:

TODAY I FEEL... A DoodlyCouch© Drawing Therapy Journal

Date:_____

How do you feel today?
Take as much time as you'd like, and either draw or write about your feelings today:

TODAY I FEEL... A DoodlyCouch© Drawing Therapy Journal

Date:_____

How do you feel today?

Take as much time as you'd like, and either draw or write about your feelings today:

TODAY I FEEL... A DoodlyCouch© Drawing Therapy Journal

Date:_____

How do you feel today?
Take as much time as you'd like, and either draw or write about your feelings today:

TODAY I FEEL... A DoodlyCouch© Drawing Therapy Journal

Date:_____

How do you feel today?

Take as much time as you'd like, and either draw or write about your feelings today:

TODAY I FEEL... A DoodlyCouch© Drawing Therapy Journal

Date:_____

How do you feel today?
Take as much time as you'd like, and either draw or write about your feelings today:

TODAY I FEEL... A DoodlyCouch© Drawing Therapy Journal

Date:_____

How do you feel today?
Take as much time as you'd like, and either draw or write about your feelings today:

TODAY I FEEL... A DoodlyCouch© Drawing Therapy Journal

Date:_____

How do you feel today?
Take as much time as you'd like, and either draw or write about your feelings today:

TODAY I FEEL... A DoodlyCouch© Drawing Therapy Journal

Date:_____

How do you feel today?
Take as much time as you'd like, and either draw or write about your feelings today:

TODAY I FEEL... A DoodlyCouch© Drawing Therapy Journal

Date:_____

How do you feel today?
Take as much time as you'd like, and either draw or write about your feelings today:

TODAY I FEEL... A DoodlyCouch© Drawing Therapy Journal

Date:_____

How do you feel today?
Take as much time as you'd like, and either draw or write about your feelings today:

TODAY I FEEL... A DoodlyCouch© Drawing Therapy Journal

Date:_____

How do you feel today?
Take as much time as you'd like, and either draw or write about your feelings today:

TODAY I FEEL... A DoodlyCouch© Drawing Therapy Journal

Date:_____

How do you feel today?
Take as much time as you'd like, and either draw or write about your feelings today:

TODAY I FEEL... A DoodlyCouch© Drawing Therapy Journal

Date:_____

How do you feel today?
Take as much time as you'd like, and either draw or write about your feelings today:

TODAY I FEEL... A DoodlyCouch© Drawing Therapy Journal

Date:_____

How do you feel today?
Take as much time as you'd like, and either draw or write about your feelings today:

TODAY I FEEL... A DoodlyCouch© Drawing Therapy Journal

Date:_____

How do you feel today?
Take as much time as you'd like, and either draw or write about your feelings today:

TODAY I FEEL... A DoodlyCouch© Drawing Therapy Journal

Date:_____

How do you feel today?

Take as much time as you'd like, and either draw or write about your feelings today:

TODAY I FEEL... A DoodlyCouch© Drawing Therapy Journal

Date:_____

How do you feel today?
Take as much time as you'd like, and either draw or write about your feelings today:

TODAY I FEEL... A DoodlyCouch© Drawing Therapy Journal

Date:_____

How do you feel today?

Take as much time as you'd like, and either draw or write about your feelings today:

TODAY I FEEL... A DoodlyCouch© Drawing Therapy Journal

Date:_____

How do you feel today?
Take as much time as you'd like, and either draw or write about your feelings today:

TODAY I FEEL... A DoodlyCouch© Drawing Therapy Journal

Date:_____

How do you feel today?
Take as much time as you'd like, and either draw or write about your feelings today:

TODAY I FEEL... A DoodlyCouch© Drawing Therapy Journal

Date:_____

How do you feel today?
Take as much time as you'd like, and either draw or write about your feelings today:

TODAY I FEEL... A DoodlyCouch© Drawing Therapy Journal

Date:_____

How do you feel today?

Take as much time as you'd like, and either draw or write about your feelings today:

TODAY I FEEL... A DoodlyCouch© Drawing Therapy Journal

Date:_____

How do you feel today?
Take as much time as you'd like, and either draw or write about your feelings today:

TODAY I FEEL... A DoodlyCouch© Drawing Therapy Journal

Date:_____

How do you feel today?
Take as much time as you'd like, and either draw or write about your feelings today:

TODAY I FEEL... A DoodlyCouch© Drawing Therapy Journal

Date:_____

How do you feel today?
Take as much time as you'd like, and either draw or write about your feelings today:

TODAY I FEEL... A DoodlyCouch© Drawing Therapy Journal

Date:_____

How do you feel today?

Take as much time as you'd like, and either draw or write about your feelings today:

TODAY I FEEL... A DoodlyCouch© Drawing Therapy Journal

Date:_____

How do you feel today?
Take as much time as you'd like, and either draw or write about your feelings today:

TODAY I FEEL... A DoodlyCouch© Drawing Therapy Journal

Date:_____

How do you feel today?

Take as much time as you'd like, and either draw or write about your feelings today:

TODAY I FEEL... A DoodlyCouch© Drawing Therapy Journal

Date:_____

How do you feel today?
Take as much time as you'd like, and either draw or write about your feelings today:

TODAY I FEEL... A DoodlyCouch© Drawing Therapy Journal

Date:_____

How do you feel today?

Take as much time as you'd like, and either draw or write about your feelings today:

TODAY I FEEL... A DoodlyCouch© Drawing Therapy Journal

Date:_____

How do you feel today?

Take as much time as you'd like, and either draw or write about your feelings today:

TODAY I FEEL... A DoodlyCouch© Drawing Therapy Journal

Date:_____

How do you feel today?

Take as much time as you'd like, and either draw or write about your feelings today:

TODAY I FEEL... A DoodlyCouch© Drawing Therapy Journal

Date:_____

How do you feel today?
Take as much time as you'd like, and either draw or write about your feelings today:

TODAY I FEEL... A DoodlyCouch© Drawing Therapy Journal

Date:_____

How do you feel today?

Take as much time as you'd like, and either draw or write about your feelings today:

TODAY I FEEL... A DoodlyCouch© Drawing Therapy Journal

Date:_____

How do you feel today?
Take as much time as you'd like, and either draw or write about your feelings today:

TODAY I FEEL... A DoodlyCouch© Drawing Therapy Journal

Date:_____

How do you feel today?

Take as much time as you'd like, and either draw or write about your feelings today:

TODAY I FEEL... A DoodlyCouch© Drawing Therapy Journal

Date:_____

How do you feel today?
Take as much time as you'd like, and either draw or write about your feelings today:

TODAY I FEEL... A DoodlyCouch© Drawing Therapy Journal

Date:_____

How do you feel today?
Take as much time as you'd like, and either draw or write about your feelings today:

TODAY I FEEL... A DoodlyCouch© Drawing Therapy Journal

Date:_____

How do you feel today?
Take as much time as you'd like, and either draw or write about your feelings today:

TODAY I FEEL... A DoodlyCouch© Drawing Therapy Journal

Date:_____

How do you feel today?

Take as much time as you'd like, and either draw or write about your feelings today:

TODAY I FEEL... A DoodlyCouch© Drawing Therapy Journal

Date:_____

How do you feel today?
Take as much time as you'd like, and either draw or write about your feelings today:

TODAY I FEEL... A DoodlyCouch© Drawing Therapy Journal

Date:_____

How do you feel today?

Take as much time as you'd like, and either draw or write about your feelings today:

TODAY I FEEL... A DoodlyCouch© Drawing Therapy Journal

Date:_____

How do you feel today?

Take as much time as you'd like, and either draw or write about your feelings today:

TODAY I FEEL... A DoodlyCouch© Drawing Therapy Journal

Date:_____

How do you feel today?
Take as much time as you'd like, and either draw or write about your feelings today:

TODAY I FEEL... A DoodlyCouch© Drawing Therapy Journal

Date:_____

How do you feel today?
Take as much time as you'd like, and either draw or write about your feelings today:

TODAY I FEEL... A DoodlyCouch© Drawing Therapy Journal

VV Date:_____

How do you feel today?
Take as much time as you'd like, and either draw or write about your feelings today:

TODAY I FEEL... A DoodlyCouch© Drawing Therapy Journal

Date:_____

How do you feel today?

Take as much time as you'd like, and either draw or write about your feelings today:

TODAY I FEEL... A DoodlyCouch© Drawing Therapy Journal

Date:_____

How do you feel today?

Take as much time as you'd like, and either draw or write about your feelings today:

TODAY I FEEL... A DoodlyCouch© Drawing Therapy Journal

Date:_____

How do you feel today?
Take as much time as you'd like, and either draw or write about your feelings today:

TODAY I FEEL... A DoodlyCouch© Drawing Therapy Journal

Date:_____

How do you feel today?

Take as much time as you'd like, and either draw or write about your feelings today:

TODAY I FEEL... A DoodlyCouch© Drawing Therapy Journal

Date:_____

How do you feel today?
Take as much time as you'd like, and either draw or write about your feelings today:

TODAY I FEEL... A DoodlyCouch© Drawing Therapy Journal

Date:_____

How do you feel today?
Take as much time as you'd like, and either draw or write about your feelings today:

TODAY I FEEL... A DoodlyCouch© Drawing Therapy Journal

Date:_____

How do you feel today?
Take as much time as you'd like, and either draw or write about your feelings today:

TODAY I FEEL... A DoodlyCouch© Drawing Therapy Journal

Date:_____

How do you feel today?

Take as much time as you'd like, and either draw or write about your feelings today:

TODAY I FEEL... A DoodlyCouch© Drawing Therapy Journal

Date:_____

How do you feel today?
Take as much time as you'd like, and either draw or write about your feelings today:

TODAY I FEEL... A DoodlyCouch© Drawing Therapy Journal

VV Date:_____

How do you feel today?
Take as much time as you'd like, and either draw or write about your feelings today:

TODAY I FEEL... A DoodlyCouch© Drawing Therapy Journal

Date:_____

How do you feel today?
Take as much time as you'd like, and either draw or write about your feelings today:

TODAY I FEEL... A DoodlyCouch© Drawing Therapy Journal

Date:_____

How do you feel today?

Take as much time as you'd like, and either draw or write about your feelings today:

TODAY I FEEL... A DoodlyCouch© Drawing Therapy Journal

Date:_____

How do you feel today?
Take as much time as you'd like, and either draw or write about your feelings today:

TODAY I FEEL... A DoodlyCouch© Drawing Therapy Journal

Date:_____

How do you feel today?

Take as much time as you'd like, and either draw or write about your feelings today:

TODAY I FEEL... A DoodlyCouch© Drawing Therapy Journal

Date:_____

How do you feel today?
Take as much time as you'd like, and either draw or write about your feelings today:

TODAY I FEEL... A DoodlyCouch© Drawing Therapy Journal

Date:_____

How do you feel today?
Take as much time as you'd like, and either draw or write about your feelings today:

TODAY I FEEL... A DoodlyCouch© Drawing Therapy Journal

Date:_____

How do you feel today?

Take as much time as you'd like, and either draw or write about your feelings today:

TODAY I FEEL... A DoodlyCouch© Drawing Therapy Journal

Date:_____

How do you feel today?
Take as much time as you'd like, and either draw or write about your feelings today:

TODAY I FEEL... A DoodlyCouch© Drawing Therapy Journal

Date:_____

How do you feel today?
Take as much time as you'd like, and either draw or write about your feelings today:

TODAY I FEEL... A DoodlyCouch© Drawing Therapy Journal

Date:_____

How do you feel today?
Take as much time as you'd like, and either draw or write about your feelings today:

TODO I FEEL... A DoodlyCouch© Drawing Therapy Journal

Date:_____

How do you feel today?
Take as much time as you'd like, and either draw or write about your feelings today:

TODAY I FEEL... A DoodlyCouch© Drawing Therapy Journal

Date:_____

How do you feel today?

Take as much time as you'd like, and either draw or write about your feelings today:

TODAY I FEEL... A DoodlyCouch© Drawing Therapy Journal

Date:_____

How do you feel today?
Take as much time as you'd like, and either draw or write about your feelings today:

TODAY I FEEL... A DoodlyCouch© Drawing Therapy Journal

Date:_____

How do you feel today?

Take as much time as you'd like, and either draw or write about your feelings today:

TODAY I FEEL... A DoodlyCouch© Drawing Therapy Journal

Date:_____

How do you feel today?
Take as much time as you'd like, and either draw or write about your feelings today:

TODAY I FEEL... A DoodlyCouch© Drawing Therapy Journal

Date:_____

How do you feel today?

Take as much time as you'd like, and either draw or write about your feelings today:

TODAY I FEEL... A DoodlyCouch© Drawing Therapy Journal

Date:_____

How do you feel today?
Take as much time as you'd like, and either draw or write about your feelings today:

TODAY I FEEL... A DoodlyCouch© Drawing Therapy Journal

Date:_____

How do you feel today?

Take as much time as you'd like, and either draw or write about your feelings today:

TODAY I FEEL... A DoodlyCouch© Drawing Therapy Journal

Date:_____

How do you feel today?
Take as much time as you'd like, and either draw or write about your feelings today:

TODAY I FEEL... A DoodlyCouch© Drawing Therapy Journal

Date:_____

How do you feel today?
Take as much time as you'd like, and either draw or write about your feelings today:

TODAY I FEEL... A DoodlyCouch© Drawing Therapy Journal

Date:_____

How do you feel today?
Take as much time as you'd like, and either draw or write about your feelings today:

TODAY I FEEL... A DoodlyCouch© Drawing Therapy Journal

Date:_____

How do you feel today?

Take as much time as you'd like, and either draw or write about your feelings today:

TODAY I FEEL... A DoodlyCouch© Drawing Therapy Journal

Date:_____

How do you feel today?
Take as much time as you'd like, and either draw or write about your feelings today:

TODAY I FEEL... A DoodlyCouch© Drawing Therapy Journal

Date:_____

How do you feel today?
Take as much time as you'd like, and either draw or write about your feelings today:

TODAY I FEEL... A DoodlyCouch© Drawing Therapy Journal

Date:_____

How do you feel today?

Take as much time as you'd like, and either draw or write about your feelings today:

TODAY I FEEL... A DoodlyCouch© Drawing Therapy Journal

Today I Feel...
A DoodlyCouch Workbook
Copyright 2009
Amy S. Morgan
Photocopying and reproduction prohibited

TODAY I FEEL... A DoodlyCouch© Drawing Therapy Journal

Illustrations by Tyler and Emma Morgan

Made in the USA
San Bernardino, CA
06 December 2017